T0288424

THE Pack IS Back

PATHFINDER EDITION

By Gary Miller and Paul Tolme

CONTENTS

Return *of the* Gray Wolf

By Gary Miller

YOU PROBABLY KNOW the story of Little Red Riding Hood. The big, bad wolf devours a little old lady—and tries to snack on her granddaughter! Stories like that helped give wolves a bad rap. Do wolves really deserve their big, bad reputation?

IN THE PAST, most people thought they did. People feared and hated wolves. There's a reason for that. Wolves are fierce predators. Their jaws can take down a moose and even crush bone. Yet the fact is that wolves rarely attack humans today. Many people today understand that wolves are an important part of the natural world.

In most of the United States, gray wolves are **endangered**. In some areas, people are working to bring wolves back. Soon, the sound of a wolf howling may echo in a wilderness near you.

Creatures in Conflict

Gray wolves are the largest wild members of the dog family. Long ago, gray wolves lived across most of North America. They stalked deer in the scorching deserts of Mexico. They chased caribou across the frozen Arctic plains.

Making a Comeback. *Once nearly extinct, gray wolves are returning to some areas of the United States.*

When Europeans first came to America, conflicts with wolves began. Wolves sometimes killed livestock such as cattle and sheep. Wolves also killed deer and other animals that people hunted for food. This made it harder for settlers to succeed. For these reasons, people tried to wipe out wolves. They used guns, traps, and poison to do the job. They even received a reward for each wolf they killed.

As you can imagine, that wasn't good news for wolves. By about 1940, there were hardly any wolves left in the U.S. outside of Alaska. Only 300 or so wolves survived. They all lived in northern Minnesota.

Survival in the wild is always a challenge. Wolves face this challenge in groups called packs. Packs hunt together and share food. This helps pack members survive.

Who's the Boss? *These wolves may look ready to rip each other to pieces. Yet they are not fighting. The wolf on the left is showing the other wolf who is the boss. A wolf pack's leaders show their dominance by standing taller than other wolves.*

Hoot and Howl

"A wolf pack is very much like a human family," says scientist L. David Mech. "It's a pair of adults and their offspring. The adults lead the pack just like human parents lead their own families."

Mech knows what he's talking about. He has studied wolves for more than 50 years. He's learned that wolves and people have more than one thing in common.

You talk to the people in your family. Wolves communicate with one another, too. How? One way is body language.

A wolf pup might lick the mouth of an adult. That's a signal that the pup is hungry. In response, the adult spits up some food. Yuck! That may sound disgusting to you. To a hungry young wolf, it's a tasty meal.

Wolves have another, famous way of communicating. They howl. Mech says that wolves howl to find each other when they get separated. They also howl to signal that it's time to hunt. In fact, the pack may gather for a big howling session before hunting. It's a lot like the pep rally before the big game!

Snack Time. *A wolf pup licks its mother's mouth to tell her it wants to eat.*

Body Language. *For wolves, touching one another is a way of saying hello.*

Pack Attack!

For wolves, hunting is serious business. To stay healthy, an adult gray wolf needs to eat at least 2.2 kilograms (5 pounds) of meat a day. A wolf can eat more than 9 kilograms (20 pounds) at a time! Wolf packs tackle many types of prey. Their favorites are large herbivores, or plant eaters, such as elk and moose.

Rolf Peterson is an expert on the way wolves hunt. "The wolf's jaws are incredibly strong," Peterson says. "They help a wolf bring down and kill prey. A wolf's brain is important, too." Wolves choose their prey carefully before attacking. That's because prey animals can fight back. A moose, for example, has huge hooves and strong legs. One kick can kill a wolf.

To avoid injury, wolves try to pick the weakest animal to attack. How do wolves know an animal is weak? Scientists aren't sure. Maybe wolves use their eyes to see if an animal is limping or moving slowly. Believe it or not, a wolf might even use its nose to smell weakness in its prey.

"The nose of a wolf is very sensitive," says Peterson. "Some dogs can smell cancer in humans. Wolves may be able to smell disease in prey animals, too."

Big Meal. *Working together in a pack, wolves can kill large animals, such as this elk.*

New Attitudes, New Hope

Chances are, you have never seen a wolf in the wild. This might soon change. In some parts of the United States, wolves are returning.

In 1973, the U.S. government signed the Endangered Species Act. This made it illegal to harm endangered species, such as the wolf. It also gave some people hope that wolves might once again roam across the United States.

Why would people want wolves to come back? Some people's feelings about wolves have changed. Long ago, most people raised livestock. They had a reason to dislike wolves. Today, fewer Americans are ranchers. That means fewer people worry about wolves killing their livestock. People have learned more about wolf behavior, too. They know that wolves hardly ever attack humans today.

People also understand more about wolves' importance. In a single day, a pack may cover 80 kilometers (50 miles) while hunting. Wolves help keep an ecosystem in balance. They do it by killing deer, moose, and other plant-eating animals. Sometimes those creatures eat too many plants. That damages the ecosystem. Wolves help reduce the number of plant eaters, making the wilderness healthier.

The Wolves Return

The Endangered Species Act of 1973 helped wolves begin their comeback. Wolf numbers in Minnesota grew. Soon wolf packs roamed across Minnesota and Wisconsin, too. Biologists helped wolves return to other areas. In 1995 and 1996, scientists released 66 wild wolves in Yellowstone National Park and nearby areas.

Yet the return of the wolves also meant a return to conflicts. Many ranchers fought against the idea. Why?

Family Ties. *A wolf pack usually has four to ten family members.*

Well, the ranchers worried that wolves would hurt their livestock. So to help the ranchers, wildlife groups agreed to pay for any livestock killed by wolves.

Here to Stay

By 2008, about 1,500 gray wolves lived in and around Yellowstone. Some people think they are even ready to come off the Endangered Species list in that area. Other groups disagree and are working to keep wolves protected.

With their numbers growing, wolves are here to stay. Gray wolf numbers in the United States are rising about 25 percent a year. As new packs form, wolves enter new areas. Keep your eyes open. On a walk in the woods, you may see a flash of gray fur. You may hear a distant howl. If you do, howl back. It's the social thing to do.

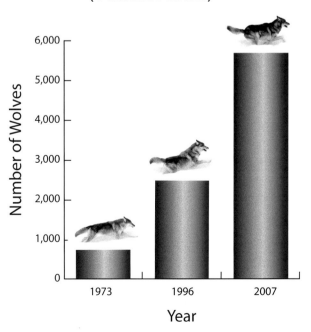

U.S. Gray Wolf Population (Outside Alaska)

Number of Wolves

6,000
5,000
4,000
3,000
2,000
1,000
0

1973   1996   2007

Year

The Pack is Back

By Paul Tolme

Wolves are making a big comeback in the United States. They are helping other animals survive.

DOUG SMITH STOOD ON A HILL in Yellowstone National Park. He looked at a wolf den, or home, through his binoculars. He moved slowly. He stayed quiet. He did not want to scare the wolves in the den. Soon a wolf came out of the den.

It was a mother wolf. She smelled the air, looking around for danger. It was safe. Then three wolf pups, or babies, followed her out of the den.

Feeling safe, the pups wrestled in the grass. Smith was glad to see the playful pups. They showed him that the number of wolves in the park is rising.

Knowing that makes Smith happy. You see, he is a wolf biologist. He is a scientist that studies the gray wolves that live in the park. Long ago, lots of wolves lived there. People killed them off because the wolves attacked livestock, like cattle and sheep, on nearby farms.

Bringing Wolves Back

Not so long ago, no wolves lived in the park. In 1995, Smith brought wolves to the park from Canada. It was the first time in 80 years that wolves lived in Yellowstone. Bringing back a plant or animal species to a place it once lived is called **reintroduction**.

Reintroduction keeps the park's ecosystem healthy. Wolves increase the park's **biodiversity**. That means they increase the number of different types of plants and animals there.

Biodiversity is important because many plants and animals depend on other types of plants and animals to stay alive.

When many species live in the same place, they depend on one another to stay healthy. If one species dies out in that place, other species may die out, too.

Wolves in Yellowstone increase biodiversity by hunting elk. Before Smith brought wolves back to the park, too many elk lived there. The elk ate all the shrubs, or small plants. Now that the wolves are back, more shrubs can grow in the park.

Shrubs are important because some animals need them. Beavers, for example, eat shrubs. Because more shrubs now grow in the park, more beavers live there, too.

Those busy beavers build dams to make ponds. Fish live in the ponds. Eagles eat the fish in beaver ponds. By eating elk, wolves have helped all these plants and animals.

Studying Wolves. *Doug Smith checks a wolf. A kind of medicine keeps the wolf still while Smith examines it.*

Growing Population. *Gray wolves, such as this one, are an endangered species. That means few gray wolves live in the United States. The number of gray wolves is growing, however. These animals may not be considered endangered much longer.*

Nosing Around. *This red wolf sniffs the ground. It might pick up the scent of a tasty raccoon.*

Leftovers

You might think that gray wolves' hunting elk is cruel. Yet Smith has learned that wolves usually hunt only sick elk. By eating sick elk, wolves make an elk herd stronger. So even elk benefit from wolves.

Other animals also benefit from wolves' elk hunting. These animals eat the parts of an elk body the wolves don't eat. Bears, birds, and foxes eat the leftover elk. That means lots of animals get a free meal.

All these leftovers are helping Yellowstone's **food web** grow. A food web shows how some species change the lives of others by what they eat. For example, by eating elk, wolves have changed life for elk, shrubs, and beavers. They have also changed the lives of fish, eagles, bears, birds, and foxes. These changes will affect other plant and animal species, too.

The Wolf Effect

All the changes that wolves make are called the **wolf effect**. It happens everywhere wolves live. For example, Smith has seen the wolf effect in the Arctic, a place near the North Pole. Wolves that live there are white. They eat rabbits and a type of deer called caribou. Rabbits and caribou eat plants. If there were no wolves, the rabbits and caribou would eat all the plants.

The wolves in North Carolina also improve their habitat. Too many raccoons lived in some parts of the state. The raccoons feasted on quail and turtles.

Before long, there weren't enough quail or turtles. Then scientists reintroduced red wolves. The wolves eat raccoons. Soon more quail and turtles lived there as well. The ecosystem is now healthier than it was before wolves came back.

Hard to See. *This Arctic wolf's white color helps it blend into its snowy surroundings.*

Chasing Wolves

Smith spends his days checking on Yellowstone's gray wolves. Sometimes he gets as close as he can. At other times, he is farther away. For example, on the same day he saw the wolf pups, Smith flew in a helicopter.

The helicopter chased a wolf running on the ground. Smith raised a dart gun. He aimed and pulled the trigger. Bull's-eye! The dart hit the wolf, putting it to sleep.

As the helicopter landed, Smith jumped out. He checked the wolf's teeth. They were sharp. He weighed the wolf. It was a good checkup. The wolf was healthy.

Finally, Smith put a special collar on the wolf. The collar gives off a radio signal. It tells Smith where the wolf is. It will help him check on the wolf wherever it roams.

Wolf packs are growing in Yellowstone. Smith is happy to help them grow strong.

Wolf Fear

Not everyone is happy about the wolf's return to North Carolina and other areas. They think that wolves will attack people. Many farmers and ranchers fear that wolves will feed on their animals.

People have some reason to fear wolves. Wolves can be dangerous. Around Yellowstone, they have attacked dogs and livestock. In some places, wolves have even attacked people.

Smith has a solution. People should scare wolves away by making loud sounds or shining bright lights. Most wolves are afraid of people. They're most likely to run away if a person comes near.

Since wolves are so afraid of people, they sometimes hide. That makes it hard to tell if reintroduced wolves are doing well in their new homes.

Wordwise

biodiversity: number of different types of plants and animals in a place

endangered: at risk of dying out

food web: how some species change the lives of others by what they eat

reintroduction: bringing back a plant or animal species to a place it once lived

wolf effect: changes that wolves cause

Join the PACK

Find out why wolves are making a big comeback. Then answer these questions.

1 Describe two methods that wolves use to communicate. Include an example for each.

2 What happened to wolf populations before 1973? What happened after 1973?

3 Name ways that wolves help the environment.

4 Where are wolves found in the U.S. today?

5 How do people feel about reintroducing wolves? Use both articles to answer.